Ribbons

The basics—**satin, sheer** and **gingham**—are traditional ribbons. Each is versatile, which keeps them at the top of everyone's list. Satin ribbons come in almost every color and width. Want some contrast? Choose double-faced satin ribbon. Sheer ribbons are romantic. Try the sheers with wire edges for shaping control. Sheers trimmed with satin offer a sophisticated touch. And don't forget the ginghams! This tiny checked pattern is always popular.

For a subtle color combination, **ombre** is the answer. Ombre ribbon features a gradient change between two colors for a soft contrast.

The most recent trend in ribbons is **textured ribbon.** Some feature patterns woven into the fabric, while others are embossed for a multi-dimensional effect. Metallic netting makes a great ribbon choice for holiday decorating.

There are a myriad of **ribbon** styles and colors available for any decorating, fashion or crafting project. Here's a quick listing of the basic and specialized ribbons available in most craft stores.

The most versatile ribbon is **grosgrain.** It's ribbed satin texture will work in any decorating, fashion or craft project. Plus it's pratically indestructable.

When you want more than a solid color, choose ribbons with **patterns** and **prints.** Most are made of satin or taffeta and feature flowers, stripes and plaids. There are also dots, checks, tie-dyed and even scenic prints are available. Look for seasonal prints in your local craft store for your holiday decorations and packages.

Satins:

Sheers:

Ginghams:

Grosgrains:

Ombre:

Patterns and Prints

Textured:

Ribbons

Bows are ribbons with personality. Each conveys a certain style. The material of the ribbon sets the tone.

Knotted

The simplest bow is the **knotted bow.** Tie a single knot in the center of the ribbon length and you're done! The wider the ribbon, the more gathered the bow. Cut each tail at an angle or an inverted "V."

knotted bow with 1½" wide navy grosgrain ribbon.

knotted bow with ⅜" wide light orchid grosgrain ribbon.

Shoestring

We've all learned how to tie a **shoestring bow** when we first learned to tie our shoes. Who knew such a basic bow could create so many different looks!

Shoestring bow with 1½" wide black gingham ribbon with wire edges.

Shoestring bow with 1½" wide blue/yellow/orange plaid ribbon with wire edges. Each tail is slightly crumpled. A ⅝" wide yellow button is glued to the bow center.

Shoestring bow with ⅛" wide white stitched black grosgrain ribbon.

Double shoestring bow with ⅜" wide light blue sheer ribbon with satin edges. Each set of tails are knotted together, 1" from the end.

Tails

A bow isn't complete without the **tails.** Cutting the tails helps prevent unraveling. For a refined look, cut an inverted "V" into the end.

For a subtle touch, cut each tail at an angle.

Loopy

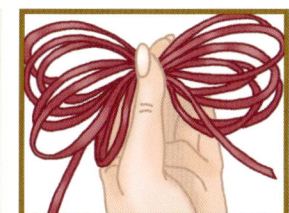
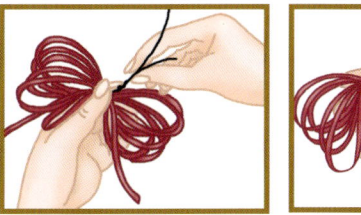

Puffy

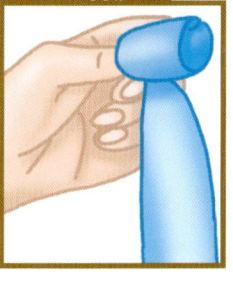

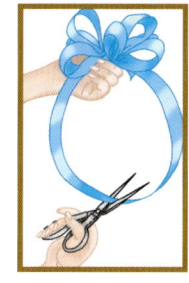

Oblong

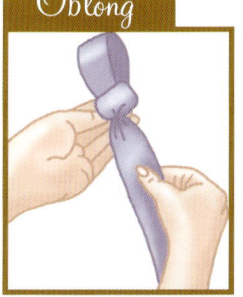

Loopy bow with ⅜" wide green sheer ribbon with satin edges.

Ribbons

Thin ribbons work best for a **loopy bow**. The delicate bow is made by crisscrossing loops on each side of your thumb, then twisting wire in the center to hold the bow in place.

Make a grand statement with a **puffy bow**. This elegant bow works well with wide ribbon. Make a center loop, form a loop on one side, twist the ribbon and form a loop on the other side, continuing for a total of ten loops. Twist wire through the center loop to secure.

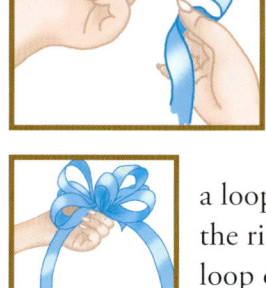

Puffy bow with 2" wide lavender sheer ribbon with wire edges.

The **oblong bow** is similar to the puffy bow, though uses different lengths for the loops.

Oblong bow with 1½" wide metallic green sheer ribbon with wire edges.

Baby

One day, you'll be tying ribbons in her hair. Why not begin with her room?

Go with grosgrain to tranform simple room decór into a magical ballet of ribbon bows and tutus. The pink grosgrain ribbon performs in many areas in this baby's room—on a wicker basket, a stuffed bear, photo frames, glass votives and a body suit.

The **wicker basket** features a 1½" wide pink grosgrain ribbon wrapped around the basket and knotted in front. The tails are trimmed to 3" with an inverted "V" cut into each end. Fill the basket with diapers, baby wipes, powder and even a change of clothes. It's a great shower gift.

One: Wash and dry the body suit. Cut the tulle in half to form two 7 yard lengths. Place the two pieces together, then fold in half lengthwise. Thread the needle, insert it into one end of the tulle, ½" below the fold. Then sew a straight stitch ½" below the folded tulle edge, gathering the fabric onto the needle. Continue gathering the entire length of tulle, then wrap it around the body suit for a proper fit.

Two: Use straight pins to attach the gathered tulle around the body suit about 3" above the snaps. Hand or machine stitch the tulle to the body suit ½" below the folded edge.

Three: Cut 8" from the pink sheer ribbon and set it aside. Sew the ribbon to the gathered tulle, twisting it twice every 1½". Sew a ribbon rose (alternating colors) along the ribbon every 1½". Cut the 8" ribbon length in half, hold the pieces together and knot them in the center. Sew the knot to the neckline. Trim each tail at an angle to 1"-1¼".

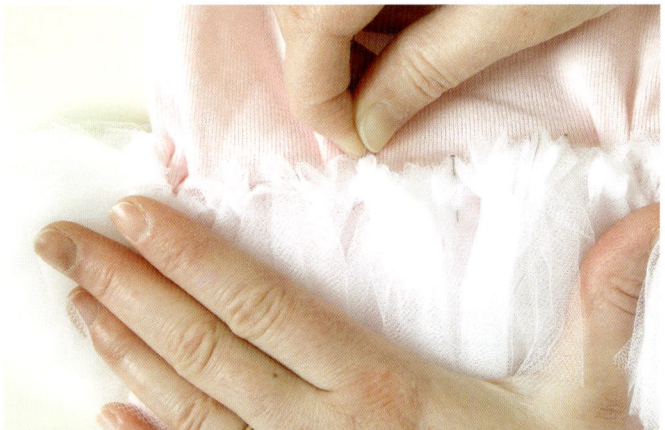

As the standard for ballerinas, a tutu can be brief (centered around the waist) or romantic (falling below the knee). A **body suit tutu** will make a delightful addition to her répertoire.

any size pink body suit
14 yards of 5⅝" wide pink tulle
1½ yards of ⅜" wide pink sheer ribbon with satin edges
⅜" wide ribbon roses with green satin ribbon leaves: 7 pink, 6 white
sewing needle
white thread
straight pins
sewing machine

Neckline Bow

(See step three)

This **ballerina bear** is ready to perform with a ribbon tulle tutu all her own.

17" tall tan plush teddy bear with movable legs
8 yards of 5⅝" wide white tulle
1⅔ yards of ⅜" wide pink sheer ribbon with satin edges
ten ⅜" wide white ribbon roses with green satin ribbon leaves
pink blush
sewing needle
white thread
low temperature glue gun
glue sticks

One: Cut 3" from the tulle and set it aside. Cut the remaining tulle in half, place the two pieces together and fold them in half lengthwise. Cut 20" from the pink ribbon and set it aside. Follow the body suit tutu steps on page five to complete the bear's tutu, then hand sew it to the bear's torso.

Two: Cut two 4" lengths from the remaining pink ribbon, hold the pieces together and knot it in the center. Glue the knot under her chin. Trim each tail at an angle to 1"-1¼".

Three: Gather the 3" tulle, pinch it in the center, then stitch with thread to secure. With the 12" ribbon length, tie a loopy bow with four 1½" loops, then stitch it to the pinched tulle. Glue the bow to her ear, then glue the ribbon rose on top. Apply blush to her cheeks.

Add a little polish to a **white body suit** with a ribbon bow and buttons. Tie a 9" length of ¼" wide pink gingham ribbon into a shoestring bow, trimming the tails at an angle. Use needle and thread to sew the bow onto the body suit collar front. Sew two ¼" wide yellow buttons below the gingham bow.

Easily cover your **photo album** with ribbons, buttons and a teddy bear to match the baby's room decór.

12"x12" blue gingham photo album
13" of 1½" wide white grosgrain ribbon
13" of ½" wide pink sheer ribbon with satin edges
2½" tall pink gingham teddy bear applique
five ⅝" wide light and dark pink buttons
white embroidery floss
fabric glue or tacky craft glue

One: Fold ½" under on each end of the white grosgrain ribbon, then glue to the album cover 2½" from the left edge. Fold ½" under on each end of the pink sheer ribbon, then glue it centered on the grosgrain ribbon.

Two: Apply the applique to the ribbon 2" from the top edge. Thread floss through each button and knot the ends at the top. Trim the ends to ⅛", then glue the buttons evenly spaced along the pink ribbon.

Photo Album

Transform **glass votives** into ballerina-themed holders. For each, use a 9" length of ¼" wide white sheer and ⅛" wide light pink satin ribbon wrapped together around the neck and tied into a bow in the front. Knot the tail ends, then glue a 1¼" tall ballet slipper or tutu button to the bow.

The ruffled trim of pink/white ombre ribbon sewed onto the cuffs of **baby socks** creates a mini tutu motif.

1 pair of white cuffed baby socks
10" of ¼" wide pink/white ombre ribbon
white thread
sewing machine or sewing needle

One: Turn the sock inside out. Cut the pink/white ombre ribbon in half. Place the ribbon on the cuff edge and stretch the cuff as much as possible while sewing the ribbon to the sock. (The cuff must be stretched as you sew to achieve the ruffled effect). Fold the ribbon ends under to finish.

Two: Repeat for the other sock. Trim any excess thread. Turn both socks right side out.

A pink grosgrain ribbon bow tops each **photo frame** for a charming look. Each frame features a 8" length of 1½" wide pink grosgrain ribbon knotted onto the center of a 16" length of pink grosgrain. Cut an inverted "V" into each of the four tails. Glue the long tails to the back of the frame. Spread each tail out to the side or hide behind the frame. For a secure mount, do not hang the frame from the the bow.

Dance

The music has started. The dance floor is clear. Now, wrap her in ribbons for this dancing dear.

- 1½" wide white grosgrain ribbon *(see step 1 for length)*
- ½" wide white elastic *(waist length plus 1½")*
- 2 yards of ⅞" wide white satin ribbon
- 3 yards of ⅜" wide pink sheer ribbon with satin edges
- 2 yards of ⅜" wide light blue sheer ribbon with satin edges
- 2 yards of ⅜" wide lavender sheer ribbon with satin edges
- 2 yards of ¼" wide light blue sheer ribbon
- 2 yards of ¼" wide iridescent ribbon
- 2" wide light blue sheer ribbon butterfly with wire and clear bead body
- sewing needle
- white thread
- 1" long safety pin
- sewing machine

Ribbons flutter and flow with movement. Attach pastel satin and sheer ribbons along a grosgrain ribbon band for a **ribbon skirt**. A blue sheer ribbon butterfly adds a crowning touch.

One: To determine the length of grosgrain ribbon for the waistband, measure the child's waist and multiply by two. To form the casing, fold the ribbon in half so it's ¾" wide, then use a sewing machine to stitch ⅛" along the long edge, leaving both ends open.

Two: Fasten the safety pin to one end of the elastic. Insert the pin into the ribbon casing, slowly scrunching the fabric as you thread the elastic through the casing. Sew each end of the elastic to the casing end, then sew the casing ends together.

Three: Cut one yard from the pink sheer ribbon and set it aside. Cut the remaining ribbons into 10"-12" lengths. Fold one end of each ribbon over ¼" and hand sew it to the inside of the waistband, alternating the ribbon styles around the waistband.

Four: Make a loopy bow with the yard of pink ribbon with six 1½" loops. Sew the bow to the center front of the waistband, then sew the ribbon butterfly to the center of the bow.

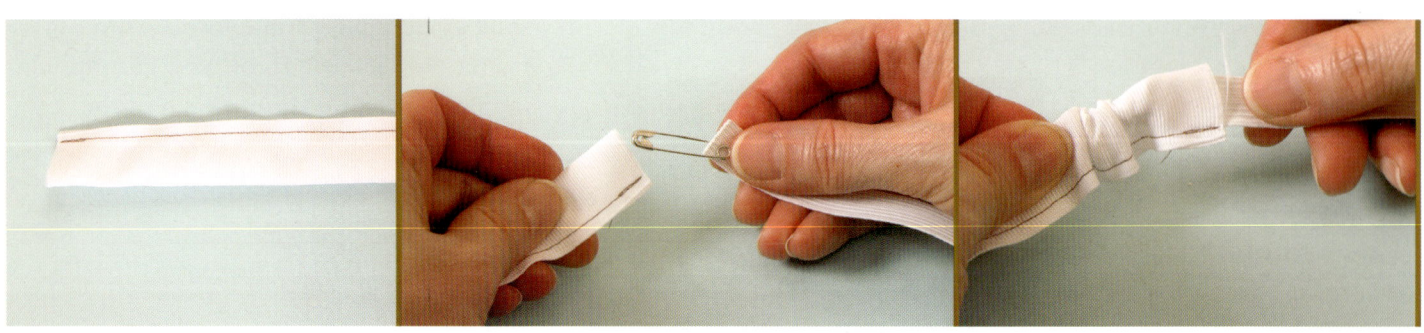

dark thread was used for demonstration purposes only

Make her dreams come true with a **ribbon wand streamer**.

2 yards of ⅜" wide blue ribbon with satin edges
1 yard of ¼" wide iridescent ribbon
18" of ⅜" wide lavender ribbon with satin edges
18" of ⅜" wide pink sheer ribbon with satin edges
2" wide light blue ribbon butterfly with wire and clear bead body
18" of ¼" wide wood dowel
white acrylic paint
½" wide paintbrush
low temperature glue gun, glue sticks

One: Paint the dowel and let dry. Cut the blue ribbon in half. Wrap one length around the dowel, gluing it every 1"-2", then glue each end in place.

Two: Hold the ends of the remaining ribbons together, then glue them to the top of the dowel. Glue the ribbon butterfly to the dowel top to cover the ribbon ends.

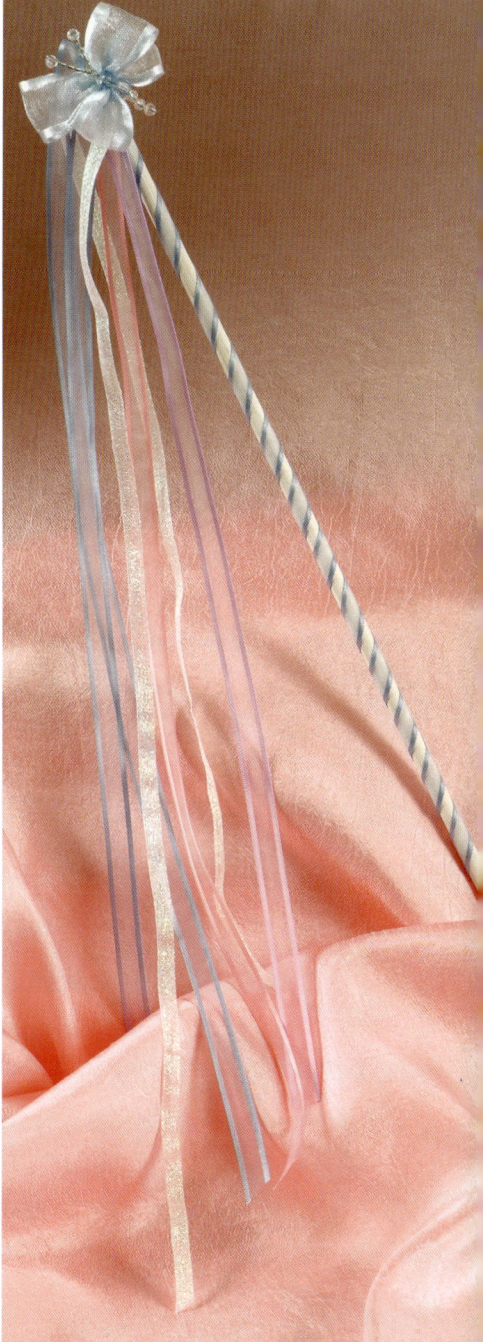

2 yards of ⅜" wide blue ribbon with satin edges
30" of ¼" wide iridescent ribbon
1½" tall porcelain angel head with hands
3¾" wide iridescent plastic angel wings
two ⅜" wide white ribbon roses with green ribbon leaves
2"x4" cardboard rectangle
sewing needle, white thread
low temperature glue gun, glue sticks

One: Cut 18" from the blue ribbon and set it aside. Wrap the remaining blue ribbon around the 4" wide cardboard, slide it off the cardboard. Cut the 18" length in half, hold both together, wrap them around one end of the loops and double-knot to form a tassel.

Two: Glue the tassel knot to the base of the angel, an arm to each side and the wings at the back. Cut 10" from the iridescent ribbon, knot the ends together and glue it to the wings back. Glue a ribbon rose on top of the knot.

Three: With the remaining ribbon, make a loopy bow with ten 1" loops. Sew the center together, then glue it to the angel front. Glue the remaining ribbon rose centered on the bow.

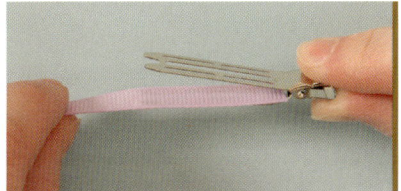

A **ribbon butterfly barrette** is just the thing to crown your dancing beauty. Use tacky craft glue to glue 9" of ⅜" wide lavender grosgrain ribbon around an alligator hair clip. Let dry, but first insert wax paper between the clip to prevent the ribbon from gluing to itself. Glue a 2" wide lavender sheer ribbon butterfly bow to the barrette top and let dry.

Birthday

Announce the important event with a **birthday banner**. It'll begin your celebration in festive style.

- 1⅔ yards of 1½" wide blue/yellow/orange plaid ribbon with wire edges
- 2⅓ yards of ⅝" wide orange gingham ribbon
- 16½"x24" rectangle of muslin fabric
- 16½" length of ¼" wide wood dowel
- eleven ⅜"–⅝" wide yellow buttons
- ½" wide fusible tape
- iron
- blue fabric paint pen
- fabric glue

One: Iron a ¾" hem along the edges of the muslin. Follow the manufacturer's directions to apply fusible tape behind the folds. Fold 1¼" of the top edge back, then use fusible tape to secure the edge, leaving a ¾" opening. Insert the dowel into the opening. Cut one yard from the orange gingham ribbon and set it aside. Double knot the ends of the remaining gingham ribbon to the ends of the dowel, then cut an inverted "V" into each ribbon end.

Two: Cut ⅔ yard from the plaid ribbon and set it aside. Cut the remaining plaid and gingham ribbons in half. Use fusible tape to apply a gingham length centered on each plaid ribbon, then use fusible tape to apply one length to the muslin below the dowel and the other 2" from the bottom edge. Glue five buttons evenly spaced along each ribbon border.

Three: Tie the remaining plaid ribbon into a shoestring bow with 2½" loops and 7" tails. Cut an inverted "V" into each tail, then glue the bow to the muslin 2½" above the bottom ribbon border. Write "Happy Birthday" with the pen on the muslin.

lollipop bows

Grosgrain ribbons add a festive touch to swirl lollipops. Wrap 8" lengths of ⅜" wide blue and orange grosgrain ribbon around the neck of the lollipop and double knot them in place. Trim each tail at an angle.

Wrap a 12" length of ⅝" wide orange gingham ribbon around a 2½" tall galvanized metal pail for a **mini favor**. Fill the pail with yellow paper crinkle and treats.

A large ribbon bow transforms a galvanized pail into a **lollipop centerpiece**. Center 1¼ yards of orange gingham ribbon onto the same length of blue/yellow/orange plaid ribbon, then wrap them around the pail and tie the ends into a bow. Cut an inverted "V" into each tail for a fun accent. Fill the pail with floral foam and yellow paper crinkle.

Give those ribbons in your hair an entirely new look with a **ribbon-wrapped headband.** Add some glue to the end of a headband, then begin wrapping a yard of ⅝" wide red/orange/white striped grosgrain ribbon around it, applying tacky craft glue every third wrap to hold the ribbon in place.

Carry all those party favors in a coordinating **denim purse.** You can use fusible tape for a quick way to apply the ribbon trim or use a sewing machine. For this 8"x10" denim purse, use 22" each of ⅝" wide red/orange/white striped grosgrain and ⅜" wide orange grosgrain ribbon for the trim plus 10" of orange gingham ribbon for the bow. And, if you happen to find one of the swirl lollipops from the party inside, don't worry—the purse is washable!

Ribbon accents make this **denim jumper** the life of the party—it even coordinates with the decorations! Measure around the hemline for the needed lengths of ⅝" wide red/orange/white striped grosgrain and ⅜" wide orange grosgrain ribbons, adding to the orange ribbon for the pocket trim. Use fusible tape or a sewing machine to apply the ribbon to the pocket. Tie 10" of orange gingham ribbon into a shoestring bow and sew it centered on the pocket ribbon. Use fusible tape or a sewing machine to apply the striped ribbon along the top of the jumper hem. Repeat the process to apply orange grosgrain ribbon along the hem bottom.

It's fun and funky. It's fashion for your room. So, dress it up with a **green charm box** and ribbon-tied **decanters** for a style all your own.

Tween Scene

- 9" of ⅜" wide yellow grosgrain ribbon
- 22" of ¼" wide red flowers on green woven ribbon
- 32" of ⅛" wide red/yellow gradient ribbon
- 3"x4½" papier mache box with scallop-edge lid
- four ¼" wide yellow flower charms with jump rings
- 12mm green glass tube bead
- acrylic paints: green, yellow, orange
- acrylic liquid sealer
- ¾" wide flat paintbrush
- tacky craft glue
- X-acto® knife

One: Apply sealer to the box and lid; let dry. Paint the box yellow and the lid green; let dry. Paint three ¾" wide orange wavy lines on each box side; let dry. Dip the paintbrush handle into the orange paint then onto the lid to make groups of three dots on the lid; let dry.

Two: Glue the woven ribbon around the lid side. Cut the gradient ribbon into quarters. Thread each length onto a charm ring, then tie the ends into a shoestring bow with ½" loops and ¾" tails. Glue a bow centered on each side of the woven ribbon. Attach the beaded handle (see box on the right) to the lid top.

bead handle

Fold the yellow ribbon in half, then thread it through the bead and pull the loop so it's 1" above the bead. Make a hole in the lid center with the X-acto® knife, then thread the ribbon (below the bead) through the hole and double knot it on the lid inside.

Spice up **glass bottles** with ribbons. Fold two 16" lengths of ⅛" wide yellow/red gradient ribbon in half. Wrap the fold around a 7" tall green wavy glass bottle and insert the ends through the fold. Thread green, clear and red 6mm glass beads onto the ribbon ends and knot the ends. Embellish a 4½" tall clear glass bottle with strips of red flowers on woven ribbon glued around the top and bottom, then wrap a 15" length of gradient ribbon around the neck; tie the ends into a shoestring bow. Tie a ¼" wide flower charm to each tail.

Wrap a **storage basket** with beaded ribbon for a creative way to organize. The versatile basket offers a canvas lining which can be washed. So, you can insert anything into the basket—towels, your hand washables, magazines or craft projects.

2⅓ yards of 1½" wide yellow/green floral ribbon with wire edges
seven assorted 12mm–15mm green glass tube beads
12"x13" wicker storage basket with canvas liner

One: Tie a knot 10" from one end of the ribbon. Thread a bead onto the opposite ribbon end, slide it up to the knot then tie a knot on each side of the bead to hold it in place. Repeat the process every 7" for the remaining beads.

Two: Wrap the beaded ribbon around the neck of the basket, then double-knot the ends to hold it in place. Trim the tails at an angle.

personalized organizer

Personalize the organizer with letters formed from yellow grosgrain ribbon. Draw the letters to size on scrap paper then measure each line to get the length of ribbon needed. To form rounded letters, make gentle pleats in the ribbon as you glue it to the organizer.

⅔ yard of ⅜" wide yellow grosgrain ribbon (plus enough for letters)
1⅓ yards of ⅜" wide sage green grosgrain ribbon
1½ yards of ⅛" wide white stitch on green grosgrain ribbon
1⅔ yards of 1½" wide green/yellow floral satin ribbon
1½ yards of 1½" wide yellow/green striped satin ribbon
19½"x30" canvas organizer
¼" wide charms with jump rings:
  4 flowers,
  2 butterflies
fabric glue

Adorn an **organizer** with ribbons and charms. Cut the floral ribbon in thirds and glue one length ¾" from the top edge of the organizer and the others between the pocket rows. Cut the striped ribbon in thirds, insert one into each metal ring along the top and tie the ends into a shoestring bow. Trim each pocket along the top and bottom rows with green ribbon and the middle row with yellow. Cut the white stitched on green ribbon into 9" lengths, thread a charm onto each, then tie each into a shoestring bow. Glue two bows on each row.

Fashion Statement

It's time to update your wardrobe with ribbons. Afterall, ribbons aren't just for hair anymore. Begin with a **timepiece** to accessorize any outfit for a style all your own!

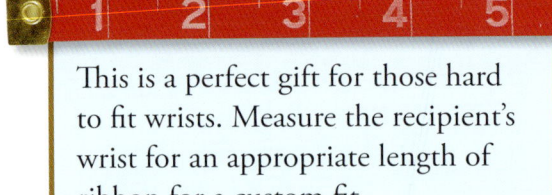

10" of ⅝" wide red/green/gold striped grosgrain ribbon
gold watch face with ⅝" wide band pins and buckle
four ⅛" wide gold eyelets
eyelet setting tools
sewing needle
red thread
black pen
X-acto® knife, cutting surface
Fray Check™ liquid

This is a perfect gift for those hard to fit wrists. Measure the recipient's wrist for an appropriate length of ribbon for a custom fit.

One: Remove the existing band and buckle from the watch (see the sidebar to the right). Place the pins back onto the watch.

Two: For the buckle end: Cut a 3½" length of ribbon. Wrap a ½" of the ribbon around the watch top pin, folding the end to the back. Use the needle and thread to sew the ribbon around the pin, forming a casing.

Three: Place the ribbon band on a cutting surface. Measure ½" from the ribbon end, then use the X-acto® knife to make a 1/16" slit in the center for a slot to insert the buckle prong. Insert the buckle prong into the cut slit, then wrap the ribbon around the buckle pin, folding the end to the back. Use the needle and thread to sew the buckle in place.

Four: Cut a 1⅜" length of ribbon, then fold it in half horizontally so it is 5/16" wide. Wrap the folded ribbon around the ribbon band so the ends meet at the back. Use needle and thread to sew the ends together (closing the overlapping ends with thread) to allow the ribbon loop to slide freely along the ribbon band.

Five: For the eyelet end: Wrap one end of the remaining ribbon around the watch bottom pin, folding ½" to the back. Use needle and thread to sew the casing in place. Place the former band onto the top ribbon band to use as a template for placing the buckle prong holes into the ribbon. Use the pen to mark each hole on the ribbon. Remove the former band and place the ribbon band on a cutting surface. Use the X-acto® knife to make 1/16" slits through each pen mark. (Note: Keep the slit small so the eyelet will not fall through the hole.) Insert an eyelet into each slit, then turn the ribbon band over and use the eyelet setting tools to secure each eyelet in place.

Finish: Trim the eyelet end at an angle. Apply Fray Check™ to each raw edge on the ribbon to protect it from fraying; let dry.

About the pins...

If your watch manual doesn't offer instructions for pin removal, we suggest taking it to a jeweler or watch repair shop to have the pins professionally removed.

Who needs all that heavy leather? Ribbons make **belts** soft and feminine. Plus, they're so easy to make, you'll want one in every color! Grosgrain ribbon is the most durable for a ribbon belt, though satin is also a great choice.

See the tip box below for measuring ribbon lengths for belts.

1½" wide ivory grosgrain ribbon
two 1¾" tall silver D-rings
sewing machine or sewing needle
ivory thread
Fray Check™ liquid

One: Hold the D-rings together and wrap one ribbon end through the rings, folding over 1¼". Machine or hand stitch the ribbon ⅛" from the straight end of the rings to form a casing.

Two: Trim the other end of the ribbon at an angle. Apply Fray Check™ to the raw edges of the ribbon to protect it from fraying; let dry.

You can make a **ribbon belt** to accent any outfit! Upon measuring the length needed, trim the ends at an angle and apply Fray Check™ to the raw edges; let dry. To wear: Wrap the ribbon through the belt loops and tie a loose knot as you'll want to be able to easily untie the knot when needed.

Tip: With all the styles from high waist to low rise pants, measure the length of ribbon through the belt loops, then add 9" to the length for the total amount of ribbon needed.

For a truly romantic look, wear a **sheer ribbon necklace** adorned with glass beads. The soft sheer ribbon adds a hint of mystery among the sparkling glass beads.

blue necklace:
42" of ¼" wide
 blue sheer ribbon
6mm glass beads
 with large
 openings:
 22 medium blue,
 13 light blue
two 5.5mm silver
 jump rings
6mm silver spring
 ring clasp
beading needle
 with large eye
tacky craft glue

white necklace:
21" of ¼" wide
 white sheer
 ribbon
ten 8mm clear
 glass triangle
 beads with large
 openings
twenty 5mm
 silver tube
 beads with large
 openings
two 5.5mm silver
 jump rings
6mm silver spring
 ring clasp
beading needle
 with large eye
tacky craft glue

For the blue necklace: Cut the ribbon to 22" and 20". Thread the 22" onto the needle, knot the opposite ribbon end 2½" from the end. Slide a dark blue, light blue and dark blue bead to the knot, then knot the ribbon again. Knot the ribbon 1" from the last knot, thread a single bead onto the ribbon, then knot again. Repeat for the remaining length of the ribbon, then repeat the process for the 20" length ribbon. Hold one of each ribbon end together and knot them onto the jump ring. Knot the two other ends onto the clasp ring. Apply glue to each knot to secure.

For the white necklace: Repeat the steps for the blue neckleace using a silver, clear and silver bead set every 1".

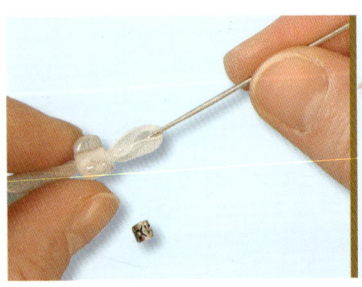 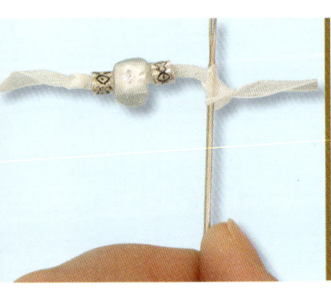 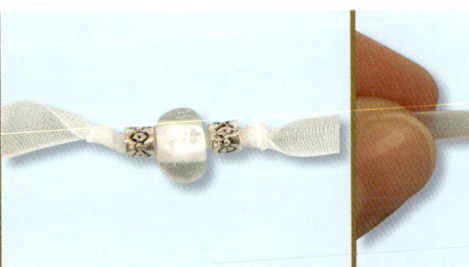 

Create romantic appeal with a **double-strand ribbon necklace.** Cut 20"–26" lengths of ⅜" wide navy and ivory sheer ribbons with satin edges. Insert one end of each ribbon through the ring on a slide or charm, pulling it to the center. Knot the ribbons together 1½" from each side of the slide. Apply Fray Check™ to the raw ends of each ribbon (to protect against fraying) and let dry.

To wear the necklaces: Wrap the ribbon ends around your neck. Tie a small shoestring bow or a loose knot to secure the ends, yet allow for ease when removing the necklace.

Make a chic fashion statement with a **sheer ribbon necklace.** Cut a 20"–26" length of 1½" wide light blue sheer ribbon. Cut one end of the ribbon at an angle and insert it through the ring on a slide or charm, pulling it to the center. Apply Fray Check™ to the raw ends of the ribbon (to protect against fraying) and let dry.

When you're not wearing your new ribbon jewelry, store it in a **blue ribbon jewelry box.** Various widths of blue grosgrain ribbon add classic charm.

12" of ⅝" wide navy blue grosgrain ribbon
32" of 1½" wide navy blue grosgrain ribbon
9"x5"x5½" unfinished wood jewelry box
Paper Pizazz® paper: *Joy's Vintage Papers* for vintage blue roses (also available by the sheet)
ivory acrylic paint
decoupage glue
1" wide foam brush
fine grain sandpaper
clean soft cloth
low temperature glue gun, glue sticks

One: Paint the inside and outside of the box and lid ivory; let dry. Lightly sand the surfaces and edges; wipe clean with a soft cloth.

Two: Tear one 3⅝"x3" and two 3⅝"x12" strips of blue roses paper. Center one of the 12" long strips onto the box front, wrapping the ends to the box sides. Apply a coat of decoupage glue over the front and box sides. Overlap the second strip ½" onto the left side of the first strip and wrap it around the back and onto the right side of the box. Apply a coat of decoupage glue to the surface. To fill the small gap on the right side of the box, decoupage the 3" long strip overlapping onto the other strips. Let dry.

Three: Tear a 7½"x4" rectangle of blue roses paper. Decoupage the rectangle centered on the lid; let dry. Apply a second coat of decoupage glue to the box and lid and let dry.

Four: Center the ⅝" wide ribbon on the lid and glue in place, wrapping the ends around the sides to the bottom. Wrap the 1½" wide ribbon around the box sides, double-knotting the ends at the center front. Cut an inverted "V" into each tail. Apply glue behind the knot, sides and back of the ribbon to hold it in place.

17

Classic

You'll always find your messages with this classic-style **message board.**

2 yards of ⅜" wide white grosgrain ribbon
1½ yards of ¼" wide black/white gingham ribbon
20" of 1½" wide black/white gingham ribbon with wire edges
10¾"x17" bulletin board with hanging hardware
9¼"x15¼" rectangle of white dots on black cotton fabric
black acrylic paint
liquid acrylic sealer
1" wide flat paintbrush
fine grain sandpaper
soft cloth
thumb tack
tacky craft glue

One: Apply sealer to the frame of the bulletin board and let dry. Paint the frame black; let dry. Lightly sand the frame, wipe the frame with a clean soft cloth, then apply sealer and let dry.

Two: Apply a line of glue around the outer edge of the cork and a few dots around the center, then place the fabric on top and smooth out.

Three: Cut the white ribbon to three 10" and one 9", 11" and 15" length. Cut the ¼" wide gingham with two 9½" and two 15½" lengths. Weave the white ribbons into a lattice pattern over the fabric, gluing the ends in place, then glue the gingham around the inside edge. Tie the wide gingham ribbon into a shoestring bow with 2¾" loops and glue the tails to the frame back. Hang the bulletin board with the hardware, then use the thumb tack to attach the bow above the frame.

Black & White—it's always a classic look.

Make your own **hurricane lamps** with glass candle holders, glass chimneys and 1½" wide black/white gingham and dots patterned ribbons. Wrap one patterned ribbon around each candle holder stem, knot it in the front, then trim the tails to 2" and cut an inverted "V" into each end. Wrap matching ribbon around a 2" tall votive candle cup, gluing the ends at the back. *(Note: Never leave a burning candle unattended.)*

Dress up a 2½"x6" pillar candle with ¼" wide white dots on black grosgrain ribbon for a striking look. Wrap an 18" length of ribbon around the candle top and tie the ends into a shoestring bow at the front. Wrap a 9" length of ribbon around the bottom, overlap the ends at the back and use a straight pin to hold it in place.

Embellish **photo frames** with black and white patterned ribbons to create depth and texture.

White-stitched black ribbon makes a striking border for a 3¾"x4¾" black photo frame. For the **wrapped frame,** glue 7" lengths of ⅛" wide white-stitched black grosgrain ribbon along the top and bottom of the frame, gluing the ribbon ends at the back. Tie a shoestring bow with a 9" ribbon length and glue it to the ribbon on the top left corner.

Embellish a plain photo mat with black/white gingham ribbon for a sensational look. For the **gingham mat,** remove the back and mat from a 5"x7" black photo frame. Cut two 5" and two 7" lengths of ⅜" wide black/white gingham ribbon. Glue the longer ribbon lengths centered along each side of the mat, then glue the 5" lengths across the top and bottom. Insert the mat with a photo into the frame, then secure the frame back.

Decorate a **votive cup** with ribbon to accessorize any spot in your home. Wrap 1½" wide white dots on black ribbon around a 2¾" tall clear glass votive cup and glue the ends at the back. Insert a candle into the cup. Since, the ribbon is on the outside of the cup, you won't have to remove the ribbon before lighting the candle.

Tip: The ribbon-wrapped candles are intended for decoration purposes only. Replace the candles with non-decorated ones before lighting.

19

Red

The color of passion and romance. Red ribbons make a definitive statement in any room. Layer them with white ribbon for a striking effect.

Layered ribbons make the perfect accessory for a **pillar candle.** Cut both ⅛" wide red satin ribbon and ½" wide white satin ribbon with sheer edges to lengths that measure 12" more than the circumference of the candle (enough for the bow). Center the red ribbon on the white, wrap it around the candle, then tie the ends into a bow. Knot each red ribbon tail, then trim both sets of tails at an angle.

Wrap a red grosgrain ribbon around a **wicker basket** for a sophisticated way to store magazines. Measure ⅝" wide red grosgrain ribbon 14" longer than the circumference of the basket (enough for the bow). Wrap it around the basket and tie the ends into a bow. Trim each tail at an angle.

Untie the ribbon to peek inside the **red ribbon box.**

15" of 1½" wide red with white dots satin ribbon
28" of 1½" wide white grosgrain ribbon
1⅓ yards of ⅝" wide red/white gingham ribbon with wire edges
4½" wide round ivory papier mâché box
5½" square of red with white speckles cotton fabric
low temperature glue gun
glue sticks

One: Place the lid upside down on the back side of the fabric square. Trace a circle ½" wider than the lid, then cut it out. Glue to the lid, pressing the edges down around the lid side.

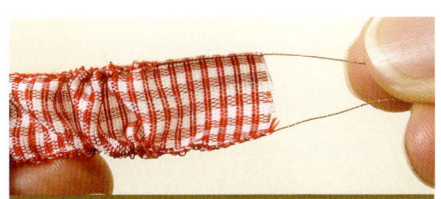

Two: Gather the red gingham ribbon to 15" by pulling the wires and scrunching the fabric. Trim the wire ends to ½" and fold under. Glue the ribbon around the lid sides.

Three: Wrap the dots satin ribbon around the box side, centered between the lid and bottom edge. Then fold the ribbon ends under and glue in place. Place the box centered on the white grosgrain ribbon, pull the ribbon to the box top and tie the ends into a shoestring bow. Trim the tails at an angle.

Red gingham on red grosgrain turns a white pillow case into a designer's dream. Place a 41" length of ⅝" wide red gingham ribbon centered on a 1½" wide red grosgrain ribbon. Center the ribbons on the sleeve of the pillow case and sew along each edge of the gingham ribbon to secure both ribbons to the case. Fold the ribbon ends under. Repeat the layered ribbons along the edge of a top sheet for a matching set.

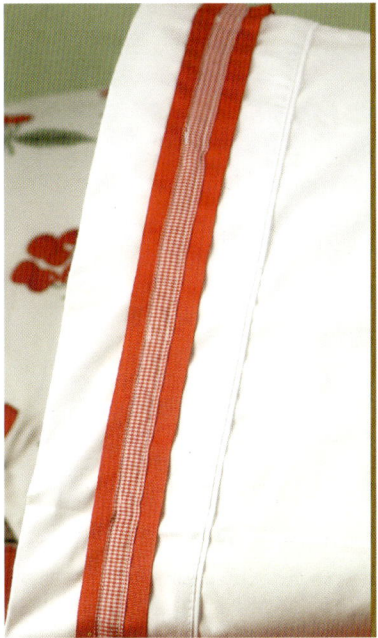

Red grosgrain ribbon ties make this **cherry pillow case** a great pick. Turn the pillow case inside out. Sew three sets of 8" long red grosgrain ribbon across from each other along the inside opening edge of the pillow case sleeve. (Use white thread, as it will not show on the outside of the pillow case.) Turn the pillow case right side out and tie each ribbon set into a bow.

Grosgrain ribbon is an excellent choice for **linens** because of its durability and washability. It's best to use wireless ribbon, as wire will bend and gather when washed.

Add a burst of color to your room with a **berries and blossoms wall planter**. This silk floral arrangement will brighten even the darkest nook. Try it hanging over a nightstand or prop it on a windowsill.

- 20" of ½" wide red/white gingham ribbon
- 5¼"x3"x7" ivory metal wall planter
- 1 stem of silk antique white wild roses with many ¾" wide blossoms, ¼" wide closed buds and 1"–1½" green leaves
- 1 stem of silk dried ivory prunus with two 10" stems of ¼"–½" wide blossoms and three 2" leaves
- 1 stem of ¾" wide red latex berries and many 1½" green leaves
- 1 silk bush of rose leaves with twelve 8"–22" long stems of ½"–1" green leaves
- 1 silk ivy bush with five 6" long stems of ½"–1" wide and three 2" long red tendrils
- 3¾"x3"x3" piece of floral foam
- two 3" long wired picks
- wire cutters
- scissors
- serrated knife
- low temperature glue gun, glue sticks

One: Use the serrated knife to cut the foam to fit inside the planter and glue in place. Cut two 14" and two 8" rose leaf stems, then curve each into a crescent. Apply glue to the stem bottoms, then insert them into the front right corner of the planter, so the stems curve along the front. Cut three 6"–8" rose leaf stems, apply glue to the stem bottoms, then insert them into the planter back left corner, extending upward. Cut the ivy stems from the bush and ten 6" rose leaf stems. Glue them along the front left, back right and center of the planter.

Two: Cut the prunus to one 10", 7" and 3" stem. Wrap a wired pick to the 3" stem. Glue the 10" stem to curve among the long rose leaf stems, the 7" to the back left and the wire-picked 3" to the back right corner, curving over the side. Cut two blossoms from the wild rose stem, then cut four 4" blossom clusters and glue them among the greenery. Glue the two blossoms to the long curved rose leaf stems. Cut the leaf sprigs from the wild rose stem and insert them among the greenery to fill empty spaces.

Three: Cut the berry stem into two 8" and five 4" sprigs. Glue one 8" sprig to extend among the long rose leaf stems and the other 8" to the back left corner. Glue the 4" sprigs among the greenery. Insert the bow pick (see inset) into the left front corner.

ribbon pick

Hold the ribbon 3½" from the end, fold it, then make a 3" loop. Repeat for three loops, then fold once more for a 3½" tail. Hold the gathered portion to the top of a wood pick and wrap the wire around it to hold it in place.

The characteristics of this **wicker basket** make it easy to wrap the ribbons through the openings of the basket weave so you don't need any glue!

24" of ¾" wide red/white checkered satin ribbon
16" of ⅝" wide red grosgrain ribbon
24" of ⅛" wide white stitches on red ribbon
24" of ⅜" wide red/white double-faced satin ribbon
16" of ⅜" wide red embossed ribbon
24" of ⅜" wide red sheer ribbon with satin edges
6"x4" white wicker basket with two 2" tall handles

Make sure to use a white wicker basket with openings along the rim to insert the ribbons. Cut each ribbon into 8" lengths. Fold one length in half, insert the fold through the opening along the rim from the inside, pulling the loop through so ½" extends out from the basket. Hold onto the loop with one hand, insert the tails through the loop and pull them down tightly to secure. Repeat with each ribbon length evenly spaced around the basket rim. Trim the tails to 2"–3", then cut the ends of each set at an angle or in an inverted "V."

Give your friends a **photo album** wrapped in ribbons and topped with a bow. It's the personal touch they'll admire along with the photos inside. Personalize the tag with your friend's name or the event or occasion depicted in the photos.

16" of 1½" wide white dots on red satin ribbon with wire edges
14" of ⅝" wide red grosgrain ribbon
14" of 1½" wide white grosgrain ribbon
14" of ⅛" wide white stitches on red ribbon
7" of ⅜" wide red/white double-faced satin ribbon
7" of ⅝" wide red/gingham ribbon
7" of ¾" wide red/white check ribbon

Paper Pizazz® *Tags Template*
cardstocks: red, white
5"x6¾" white photo album
4" of white thread
1/16" hole punch
fine point black pen
low temperature glue gun, glue sticks

One: Cut a 7" length of the dots ribbon. Fold ½" under on each end then glue the ribbon to the outer binding of the album, folding the ends to the inside. With the remaining dots ribbon, make a shoestring bow with 1½" loops and tails. Cut an inverted "V" into each tail, then set the bow aside.

Two: Cut the 14" ribbons in half. Wrap the red and white grosgrain ribbons alternating on the front cover, gluing the ends on the inside. Wrap the red/white check ribbon between the red and white grosgrains on the left side, then the gingham along the right edge, gluing the ends to the inside. Glue the stitches ribbons centered on the white grosgrain and the white side of the double-faced ribbon to the center red grosgrain. Cut a 4⅞"x6½" piece of white cardstock and glue it to the inside front cover to conceal the ribbon ends.

Three: Use the template to cut an oval tag from white cardstock, mat it on red cardstock with a thin border, then punch a hole at one end. Write "My Friends" or another message on the tag, then tie the thread onto the tag and knot the ends. Glue the knot to the bow back, then glue the bow to the album cover.

Dining

Trim a towel, embellish a tablecloth or tie your place setting together with grosgrain ribbons for tasteful highlights to your dining room decór.

2⅔ yards of ¼" wide brown/tan gingham ribbon
1 yard of ⅜" wide brown woven ribbon
7¾"x6"x4¾" wood basket with 4" tall handle
two ¾" wide tan with brown stripes buttons
low temperature glue gun, glue sticks

One: Cut 24" from the gingham ribbon, then tie a knot in the ribbon every two inches. Glue the knotted ribbon centered along the basket handle. Knot the woven ribbon every 2", wrapping it around the basket top sides and gluing it in place.

Two: Cut the remaining gingham ribbon in half. With each length, make a loopy bow with ten 1½" loops and two 1½" tails. Glue a button to the center of each bow, then glue a bow to the base of each handle.

Add an elegant touch to your dining experience with a **ribbon trimmed towel.** Cut 21½" lengths of ⅜" wide tan and ⅝" wide brown/tan striped grosgrain ribbons. Machine or hand stitch the ribbons along one end of a 20½"x28" cotton towel, wrapping ½" around each side. (Sewing prevents the ribbon from separating with frequent washings.)

Update a plain **linen tablecloth** with grosgrain ribbon for a sophisticated look in any dining room. For a 104"x70" tablecloth, you'll need 10 yards of ⅜" wide brown grosgrain ribbon. (Otherwise, double the length and width of the tablecloth, add the two measurements together, plus four more inches.) Cut the ribbon 1" longer than each side of the tablecloth. Use ¼" wide fusible tape to attach the ribbon 3" from the edge along one side of the tablecloth, wrapping ½" of the ribbon end to the back. Repeat the process for each side of the tablecloth, so the ribbons intersect in

Pull a pair of **ribbon tied curtain panels** closed and you won't mind what the weather's like outside. The ribbon ties make it easy to attach the curtain to the rod.

For a 54" wide curtain panel set and ⅝" wide rod:

7 yards of ⅜" wide tan grosgrain ribbon (fourteen 18" lengths)
fourteen ½" wide tan/ivory buttons
sewing needle
ivory thread

Fusible tape is great for quickly attaching ribbons to ornamental linens. Follow the manufacturer's directions for ironing the tape to fabric.

One: Cut the ribbon into 18" lengths. Fold one length in half, place the fold ½" below the top edge of the curtain back left corner and the button in the same corner on the curtain front. Thread the needle, insert it through the ribbon at the curtain back, push it through to the button holes on the curtain front and reinsert the needle into another button hole, pulling to the curtain back. Repeat to secure the button and ribbon firmly onto the curtain. Repeat the process for another ribbon and button every 5" along each curtain panel top.

Two: Knot each set of ribbon tails around the rod, then tie each set of ends into a shoestring bow. Trim each tail at an angle.

Garnish your **place setting** with ribbons for a striking effect. For a 19"x13" placemat, use ½" wide fusible tape to attach 20" lengths of ⅝" wide brown/tan striped grosgrain ribbon along the top and bottom, folding ½" back at each end.

Spread the ribbons apart to highlight each layer.

Ribbon napkin holders make formality fun. To wrap up a cloth napkin, cut 12" lengths of tan, brown and brown/tan striped grosgrain ribbons. Place a folded napkin (fold in quarters, then roll in thirds) centered on all three ribbons. Hold the ribbons together and double-knot the ends at the front. Trim each tail to 1½". Cut an inverted "V" into the striped tails and trim the other tails at an angle.

Ribbons add a finishing touch to this **tan floral centerpiece**.

- 1½ yards of 1½" wide ivory sheer ribbon with wire edges
- 1½ yards of ⅛" wide black squares on brown satin ribbon
- 1 bush of silk peach/brown hydrangeas with ten 4"–5" wide blossoms with many 3" leaves
- 3 stems of silk ivory roses, each with one 3" and one 2" wide blossom and one ½" wide closed bud
- 2 stems of silk ivory/pink orchids, each with many 1½" wide blossoms and ¼" wide closed buds
- 1 green silk bush of rose leaves with twelve 8"–12" long stems of ½"-1" leaves
- 1 green silk ivy bush with thirteen 7"–10" sprigs of ½"–1½" leaves and 4" long tendrils
- 2 stems of tan/brown berries, each with 4"–6" long sprigs of ⅜"–½" wide berries
- 5½"x7" copper pot with two 2" tall handles
- two 3"x4"x8" blocks of floral foam
- serrated knife
- 24-gauge wire
- wire cutters
- fifteen 3" long wood picks

One: Cut the foam to fit snuggly inside the pot. Cut the hydrangea to one 10", four 8½", one 7" and four 5½" stems. Glue the 10" stem to the pot center with the 8½" stems evenly spaced around it. Glue the 7" stem to the center front, extending downward. Glue one 5½" stem to the right of the 7" stem, then glue the three remaining stems to the left and right back of the pot. Wire the leaf stems onto the wood picks (see inside the back cover), then insert the picks around the pot center and sides.

Two: Cut two rose stems to 10", each with two blossoms and one bud. Glue the stems to the center front and left side. Cut an 8" rose stem and glue to the back right. Cut the bud stem to 7" and glue to the back left.

Three: Cut the berry stems to four 10"–14" sprigs, each with two 3"–5" sprigs. Glue the berries evenly spaced among the greenery. Cut the orchid stems to four 12" stems, each with two 6" sprigs. Glue an orchid stem to the front and back of the center hydrangea and the remaining stems around the sides to fill empty spaces.

Four: Cut the rose leaves and ivy leaves stems from the bushes. Wire one 10" and one 12" stem from each bush to a wood pick. Insert the picks into the center front, extending downward in a curve. Wire six of the taller leaf stems to wood picks, then insert the picks among the 8½" hydrangeas. Insert the remaining stems around the pot sides, extending downward.

Five: Hold the ribbons together and make a puffy bow with a center loop, six 3" loops, 4" tails for the ivory ribbon and 6" tails for the brown ribbon. Tie a knot 1" from the end of each brown ribbon tail, then cut an inverted "V" into each ivory ribbon tail. Wire the bow to a wood pick, then insert the pick into the center front of the pot.

A **ribbon-trimmed lampshade** is an enlightening way to decorate your dining room.

2½ yards of ¼" wide brown/tan gingham ribbon
11¾"x7½" white or ivory lampshade
twenty ⅜" wide tan/brown buttons
low temperature glue gun, glue sticks

Cut the ribbon into ten 8½" lengths. Wrap one length onto the **lampshade,** folding ½" on each end to the inside and glue to secure. Repeat with the remaining ribbon lengths, spaced 1¾" along the top and 3¾" along the bottom edge. Glue a button to the top and bottom of each ribbon length.

Surprise your guests with a floral **gift box** at your next dinner party.

for each gift box:
18" of ⅝" wide brown/tan striped grosgrain ribbon
1 yard of ¼" wide brown grosgrain ribbon
1½"x1½"x2½" papier mâché box
Paper Pizazz® *Tags Template*
white cardstock
1½" wide tan/peach silk hydrangea blossom
two 1" wide ivory silk wild rose blossoms
six 1"–1½" brown/green silk ivy leaves
3" of gold thread
1/16" hole punch
fine tip black pen
low temperature glue gun, glue sticks

One: Insert a gift into the box and replace the lid. Cut the brown ribbon in half. Sandwich the striped ribbon between the two brown ribbon lengths, place the box centered on the ribbons, then pull the ends above the lid and knot in place. Trim the tails to 2".

Two: Glue the flower blossoms to the knot, then glue the leaves extending outward from beneath the blossoms. Use the template to trace a small tag onto the cardstock, cut out the tag and punch a hole at the top. Use the pen to personalize the tag, then thread it onto the thread, knot the ends and glue the knot under a blossom. Place the box at a table setting.

Invite your guests to your table with a **candy jar place card** for a sweet sitting arrangement.

for each place card jar:
22" of ⅛" wide brown gingham ribbon
27" of ⅛" wide black squares on brown satin ribbon
2"x3½" clear glass jar with metal latch
2⅛"x4" ivory tag
6" of gold thread
fine tip black pen
glue stick
chocolate candy

One: Tear 2" from the bottom of the tag, then use the pen to personalize it. Cut 2⅛" of black squares ribbon and glue it to the tag bottom. Cut 9" of gingham ribbon and make a shoestring bow with ½" loops and 1" tails. Glue the bow to the tag bottom.

Two: Fill the jar with candy, then close the latch. Hold the remaining ribbons together, wrap them around the jar neck and tie the ends into a shoestring bow with 1" loops and 2" tails. Thread the tag onto the thread, then tie the thread onto the jar. Place the jar at a table setting.

Bath Accessories

Open a present each time you bathe when you dip into the **bath salts jar**. Add the salts to your bath with a ribbon-adorned scoop.

28" of 1½" wide green/pink/white plaid ribbon with wire edges
16" of ¼" wide pink/white ombre ribbon
4¼"x5" square glass jar with lid
7" long silver metal scoop
1 wired stem of two ⅝" wide pink silk flowers, one ½" tall pink berry cluster and one ¾" green leaf
28 oz. of pink bath salts
26-gauge wire
wire cutters
Glue Dots™

One: Make a puffy bow from the plaid ribbon with a center loop, eight 2" loops and two 4½" tails. Place a Glue Dot™ under the bow and press it to the center of the lid. Wrap the tails to the lid inside and use Glue Dots™ to hold them in place. Fill the jar with bath salts and place the lid on the jar.

Two: Make a loopy bow from the ombre ribbon with eight 1" loops and two 3" tails. Secure the bow to the handle base with a Glue Dot™. Wrap the bow tails to the handle back and knot the ends, then trim the ends at an angle to 1½". Cut the flowers, berry cluster and leaf from the stem. Use Glue Dots™ to attach the leaf to the lower left of the bow, the berry cluster to the upper right and the blossoms overlapping in the center.

A **ribbon trimmed towel** is the perfect accessory for a bath. Measure the width of the towel for the length of the ⅝" wide striped grosgrain ribbon. Hand or machine stitch the ribbon to the towel along the ribbon edge. Cut 9" lengths of pink grosgrain ribbon for each bow. (Note: Cut three lengths for a hand towel, five–six for a bath towel.) Tie each length into a shoestring bow with 1" loops and 1½" tails. Hand stitch each bow to the striped ribbon spaced 4" apart.

small tin:
13½" of ⅝" wide green/red/pink striped grosgrain ribbon
18" of ⅜" wide pink grosgrain ribbon
13½" of 1½" wide green/pink/white plaid ribbon with wire edges
4"x5" white tin pail
Glue Dots™ or E6000 glue
assorted green, pink and white bath accessories

One: Wrap the striped ribbon around the neck of the tin and secure the ends in back with a Glue Dot™. (Note: Glue Dots™ can be easily removed, so you can change the ribbons whenever you like.) For a permanent adhesive, use E6000 glue and work in a well-ventilated area.

Two: Wrap the plaid ribbon around the bottom of the tin and secure the ends in the back with a Glue Dot™. Wrap the pink grosgrain ribbon around the plaid ribbon and knot the ends in the front. Trim each tail at an angle to 1½".

Three: Insert bath accessories into the pail, selecting items that coordinate with the ribbons.

large tin:
22" of ⅝" wide green/red/pink striped grosgrain ribbon
26" of ⅜" wide pink grosgrain ribbon
40" of 1½" wide green/pink/white plaid ribbon with wire edges
7"x7⅜" white tin pail with 4½" metal handle
Glue Dots™ or tacky craft glue
assorted washclothes: green, pink and white

Organize your bathroom items in **ribbon tied tins** for a stylish look. Use the small tin for those smaller items, and the larger tin for wash clothes or hand towels. To decorate the large pail, wrap pink gingham ribbon around the top and striped gingham ribbon around the bottom, securing them as shown in step one of the small tin. Wrap the plaid ribbon around the center of the tin, then tie the ends into a shoestring bow with 2½" loops and 3½" tails. Cut an inverted "V" into each tail, then bend each tail slightly extending out to the sides. Fill the tin with rolled wash clothes or hand towels. (Note: To make the towels peek out further, place scrunched tissue paper or a few older wash clothes in the pail.)

Desktop

What a lovely way to coax someone to write. This **note box with note cards** will inspire any procrastinator.

2⅛ yards of ⅜" wide pink/green striped satin ribbon
1 yard of ⅛" wide white stitches on green ribbon
Paper Pizazz® papers: 2 sheets of 12"x12" green sponged paper (by the sheet); light green alphabet tiles (by the sheet)
white cardstock
9"x6½"x2¼" white cigar box
pink decorating chalk
glue stick

One: For the box: Tear an 8½"x6" rectangle from the corner of a green sponged sheet. From the remaining paper, tear two 2"x12" strips and one 2"x8" strip. Center one 12" strip along the front, wrapping the ends to each side and glue in place. Continue with the other strips around the box. Glue the rectangle centered on the lid.

Two: Tear a 4¾"x2" strip of white cardstock and chalk the edges pink. Glue the alphabet tiles to spell "NOTES" onto the cardstock, alternating angles. Glue the cardstock centered on the lid.

Three: Cut a 3½" length of striped ribbon, knot it in the center, trim each end at an angle, then glue it centered on the top of the chalked cardstock. Cut two 20" lengths of striped ribbon. Fold and glue ½" of one ribbon end to the inside front of the box, 1½" from the left edge. Wrap and glue the ribbon along the front, across the bottom, up the back, onto the lid, folding the other end to the lid inside. Repeat for the right side of the box. Cut the remaining striped ribbon in half. With each length, make a shoestring bow. Glue the bows as shown.

Four: For the note cards: Cut three 4"x12" strips from the remaining green sponged paper. Fold each strip in half to form a 6"x4" card. Cut the green ribbon into three 6" lengths and three 9" lengths. Glue one 3" length onto each card front, ¾" below the top edge. With the 9" lengths, make a shoestring bow with ½" loops and ¾" tails. Trim each tail at an angle. Glue one bow to the left end of each ribbon border on the card front. Insert the note cards into the box.

Accent a **green pillar candle** with ribbons and beads for a decorative addition to your desktop. Wrap 14" lengths of ⅜" wide pink/green striped satin and ⅛" wide white stitches on green grosgrain ribbons around the candle center and double-knot the ends in the front. Thread one clear and one green 6mm glass beads onto each grosgrain ribbon tail, then knot the tails to hold the beads in place. Trim each striped ribbon tail at an angle. (Note: slide the ribbons off before burning the candle.)

Create a special **keepsake box** with ribbons and charms. Your recipient will admire it as much as the gift inside.

1 yard of ¼" wide white stitches on green ribbon
1½ yards of ⅜" wide pink/green striped satin ribbon
3"x3"x1½" papier mâché box
½" wide silver charms: "Dancing Queen" crown with pink rhinestones, green shoe with pink rhinestone
lime green acrylic paint
½" wide flat paintbrush
liquid acyrlic sealer
low temperature glue gun, glue sticks

One: Apply sealer to the box inside and outside; let dry. Paint the box (not the lid) green inside and outside; let dry.

Two: Cut two 3½" lengths from each ribbon. Wrap a striped length around two opposite sides of the lid (flush with the edge), with the ends extending around the corners. Glue the stitched ribbon along the bottom edges of the striped ribbon.

Three: Cut six 5" lengths from each ribbon. Glue alternating ribbons to the top edge of the lid so they align with the striped ribbon on the lid side, wrapping the ends around the lid to the inside. Place the lid on the box, then place the box on the remaining striped ribbon pull the ends to the top and knot once. Slide a charm on each end up to the knot, then tie the ends into a shoestring bow. Trim each tail at an angle.

Dress up your thoughts in a **ribbon-trimmed journal.** Remove the cover from the wire binding to glue the green sponged paper to the top. Punch holes through the paper to reinsert the wire binding. Cut 4¼" lengths of each ribbon and glue them along the left side of the cover, gluing the ends to the inside. Place the cover back onto the wire binding. Hold the remaining ribbons together, wrap them around the top wire loop, thread on the medallion charm, then tie the ends into a shoestring bow with 1½" loops and 3" tails. Knot the remaining charms onto the green ribbon ends. Knot the striped ribbon ends.

18" of ⅜" wide pink/green striped satin ribbon
18" of ⅛" wide white stitches on green grosgrain ribbon
3¾" square spiral bound journal
Paper Pizazz® green sponged patterned paper
½" wide silver charms: green purse with pink rhinestones, pink martini glass, "celebrate life" medallion
⅛" hole punch
glue stick

Wedding

How could the wedding go on without ribbons? Let them join together with flowers for a romantic union.

3⅓ yards of 2½" wide white sheer ribbon with wire edges
2 yards of 1¼" wide pink sheer ribbon
4" wide white/pink silk rose with three clusters of 2½" long leaves
two 10"-12" long silk green ivy sprigs with many ½"–1½" leaves
6½" tall clear acrylic pew bow clip
white cloth covered 24-gauge wire
wire cutters
low temperature glue gun, glue sticks

One: With the white ribbon, make a puffy bow with ten 4" loops and two 17" tails. Cut an inverted "V" into each tail. With the pink ribbon, make a puffy bow with six 3" loops and two 16" tails. Cut an inverted "V" into each tail, then knot each tail 3" from the end. Wire the pink bow to the center of the white bow.

Two: Cut the rose stem to ½". Cut the leaf clusters from the stem. Glue the rose to the pink bow center. Glue the leaf clusters behind the rose as shown. Glue the ivy stems to the bow back so they hang behind the ribbon tails.

Three: Wire the bow to the plastic extension on the top of the pew bow clip. Place the clip over the end of the pew.

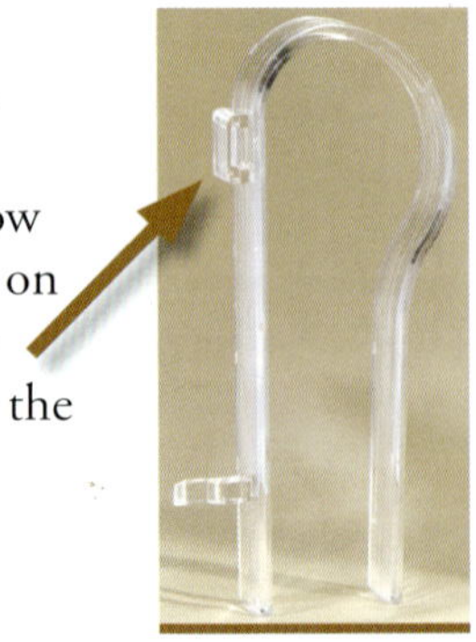

cloth covered wire:

Use cloth covered wire to secure ribbon bows. It's visually more pleasing than the stark metal sheen of traditional wire and won't cut into delicate sheer ribbons.

Tip: For a tradition pew bow with larger loops, purchase at least five yards of ribbon for each bow. Making the bows yourself is a great cost-saving measure.

The **tosser bouquet** is a silk or smaller floral rendition of the bride's bouquet. After the ceremony, the bride "tosses" the bouquet into a group of single females to signify the next "future bride."

2 yards of ⅞" wide white satin ribbon
2 stems of pink/peach/ivory silk hydrangeas, each with one 4" wide cluster of 1¼" wide blossoms
2 stems of pink/white silk roses, each with one 4" blossom, one 2" open bud and 2½" wide leaves
1 stem of white silk baby's breath with three stems of 3"–4" sprigs of many ¼" wide blossoms
6" of green 24-gauge wire or twine
wire cutters

One: Cut each of the floral stems to 8", removing the leaves below 7". Hold the hydrangea clusters together, then place one rose blossom to the front and the other to the back. Place one rose bud to the right front of the bouquet and the other bud to the left side of the bouquet. Insert the baby's breath stems between the hydrangeas and around the outside of the bouquet. Place the leaves around the outside of the bouquet. To secure the stems together, wrap the wire around the top portion of the stems and double-knot the ends. Cut off the ends of the wire.

Two: Wrap the center of the ribbon around the stem bottoms and knot it in front.

Three: Wrap the left ribbon tail around the left side of the bouquet and the right tail around the right side, pulling both upward. Crisscross the tails in the back and wrap them to the front, continuing the process up the stems to the top. When you reach the top of the stems, wrap the ribbon ends from the front to the back, next to the front again, then tie the ends into a shoestring bow with 2" loops and 8" tails. Trim each tail at an angle, then tie a knot into each tail, 1½" from each end.

A symbol of your union, the **unity candle** is a traditional part of the wedding ceremony. The bride's parents light one taper candle, while the groom's parents light the other. Each couple lights the pillar candle with their taper candle, then they extinguish the tapers.

28" of 1½" wide white satin ribbon
3 yards of ¼" wide white satin ribbon
two 12" tall dripless white taper candles
3"x9" white pillar candle
8" wide white resin candle holder for two taper candles and one pillar candle

One: Wrap the wide ribbon around the center of the pillar candle and tie the ends into a shoestring bow with 2" loops and 3" tails. Cut an inverted "V" into each tail.

Two: Cut the thin ribbon in half. Center one length 2" below the top of a taper candle, wrap each tail to the back, crisscross the ends then bring each end around to the front and repeat the process down the candle to 1½" above the bottom edge with the ends at the front. Tie the ribbon ends into a shoestring bow with ¾" loops and 1" tails. Cut each tail at an angle. Repeat the process for the second taper candle.

Note: Do not allow the taper candles to burn for more than a few minutes.

By using embossed papers, you can make **personal announcements** with your computer, printer and ribbons. Wrap two 12" lengths of ⅜" wide sheer moss green ribbon with satin edges around the bottom of the card, 1" apart, gluing the ends at the front without attaching them to the card. Tie a 10" length of ribbon around the center front of the two ribbons, then tie the ends into a shoestring bow. Cut the tails at an angle.

Purchase **embossed "Thank You" cards** and trim them with ribbon for a fanciful touch. Wrap a 12" length of ⅜" wide sheer moss green ribbon with satin edges around the bottom of the card front, gluing the ends to the card at the front. Tie a knot in the center of a 7" length of 1½" wide moss green satin ribbon and glue it to the card as shown.

The flickering light of a candle is all the more romantic through sheer ribbons.

Set the tone for romance with **sheer ribbon candle holders.** Place a white votive candle into three 2½" tall clear glass votive cups, then place one cup inside a 7½" tall clear glass cylinder vase. Wrap four 12" lengths of 2" wide ivory sheer ribbon around the cylinder vase, gluing the ends at the back. Wrap a 20" length of 1½" wide pink sheer ribbon around the top of the vase, knotting the ends in front, then cutting an inverted "V" into each tail. Repeat the ribbon motif for votive cups by wrapping a 7½" length of ivory ribbon around the cup, then tying a 12" pink ribbon length around the center.

1 yard of 1½" wide ivory sheer ribbon with satin edges
4½"x5½" clear glass ivy bowl
two 1¼" ivory satin roses
1½" wide ivory satin rose with a pearl center and two 1½" white silk leaves
clear flat-backed marbles
2" tall clear glass votive cup
white votive candle
low temperature glue gun, glue sticks

Wrap the ribbon around the **ivy bowl** and tie the ends into a shoestring bow with 2½" loops and 6" tails. Cut an inverted "V" into each tail. Cut the leaves from the blossom. Glue the satin roses to the bow center, then glue a leaf behind the blossoms, extending to each side. Insert the candle into the votive, then insert the votive inside the ivy bowl. Gently pour the marbles around the votive.

Light a **floating candle** to create a romantic setting. Place clear flat-backed glass marbles into an 8" wide shallow glass bowl, fill it ¾ full with water, then place a 3" wide floating candle in the water. Place the bowl on a 14" square beveled mirror tile for added reflective qualities. Loop 2½ yards of ⅜" wide pink sheer ribbon with satin edges around the bowl, then scatter yellow and pink silk rose petals around the bowl.

Favors are tokens of your appreciation for your guests.

for each bag favor:
three 2½"x3" white papier mâché shopping bag with 2" tall handles
low temperature glue gun, glue sticks

for the pink bag favor:
22" of 1¼" wide pink sheer ribbon with iridescent edges
9" of ⅜" wide pink sheer ribbon with satin edges
9" circles of tulle: 1 pink, 1 white
⅝" wide paper roses with ¾" green leaves: 2 pink, 1 white

for the periwinkle blue bag favor:
3½" of 1½" wide periwinkle blue satin ribbon
six 1⅞"x2¼" periwinkle blue silk and sheer rose petals
2½" tall pearl bubbles bottle with a 1⅛" wide butterfly on the lid
1" wide silver embossed double hearts circle sticker

for the green bag favor:
10" of 1½" wide moss green satin ribbon
11" of ⅜" wide green ombre ribbon
two 9" circles of white tulle
3" tall champagne bubbles bottle candy

For romance, it's the **pink bag**. Glue a 10" length of the wide ribbon around the bag center. With the remaining ribbon, tie a shoestring bow with 1¾" loops and 2½" tails. Cut an inverted "V" into each tail. With the thin ribbon, tie a shoestring bow with 1" loops and 3" tails. Knot each tail. Glue the bows together, centered on the bag front. Glue the roses centered on the bows. Insert a gift and tulle inside the bag.

For elegance, it's the **periwinkle blue bag**. Cut an inverted "V" into one end of the ribbon. Place the ribbon on the bag front, wrap the uncut end to the bag inside between the handles and glue in place. Attach the sticker to the ribbon. Insert the petals and bottle inside the bag with some petals extending upward around the bottle.

For a celebration, it's the **green bag**. Glue the wide ribbon around the center of the bag, folding the ends over to slightly overlap on the left side. Tie a knot in the narrow ribbon, 3" from the left end. Glue the knot centered on the bag front, then glue the left end around the side. Wrap the right end around the right side and back of the bag, so the ends overlap. Place the tulle circles in the bag, fill with candy, then insert the bottle on top so it extends out of the bag.

The traditional flower girl basket is filled with fresh or silk flower petals.

During the ceremony, the flower girl strolls down the aisle before the bride dropping the flower petals along the way.

20 yards of 6" wide white tulle (from a spool)
2 yards of ⅝" wide pink sheer ribbon with iridescent edges
42" of ⅜" wide pink striped sheer ribbon
1 yard of ⅛" wide pink satin ribbon
10"x4½"x5" white wicker basket with a 5" tall handle
sewing needle
white thread
low temperature glue gun, glue sticks

Purchase tulle on a roll for an economical and easy way to use this feminine material.

gathering the tulle:

Thread the needle with white thread, pull the ends even and knot the end. Insert the needle into one end of the tulle, 1" below the top edge and proceed inserting the needle in and out along the top edge of the tulle, pushing the tulle onto the needle as you go.

One: Gather the tulle (see the step box to the left) to 30". Glue the gathered tulle around the basket top edge, beginning and ending at the base of a handle.

Two: Glue one end of the pink sheer ribbon to the tulle on the handle base. Loop and lightly twist the ribbon every 2", gluing it in place. Cut 18" from the striped ribbon. Glue one end of the ribbon to the inside of the handle base, wrap the ribbon around the handle, gluing the end to the inside of the other handle base.

Three: Cut the satin ribbon in half. Hold both lengths together with the remaining striped ribbon and make a shoestring bow with 1½" loops and 7"–9" tails. Knot each tail ½"–¾" from the end. Glue the bow centered on a handle base.

Gift Wrapping

Think outside the box! Make a **gift bag** for an elegant way to present your gift.

for the ivory bag:
10" of 1½" wide ivory sheer ribbon with satin edges
1 yard of ⅜" wide purple sheer ribbon with satin edges
2 yards of 54" wide ivory tulle
two 6"x8" rectangles of purple tulle
20" of 3mm white fused pearls
8"x10" ivory gift bag with handles
white cloth-covered 24-gauge wire
wire cutters
low temperature glue gun, glue sticks

Fold the pearls in half twice then wire the fold to the gathered center of the purple tulle and glue to the top left of the **ivory bag.** Use the ivory ribbon to make a puffy bow with no center loop, six 3" loops and 8" tails, then glue to the center of the tulle bow. Use the purple ribbon to make a loopy bow with a center loop, six 1½" loops and 6" and 8" tails, then knot each tail. Glue the bow to the ivory bow center. Insert a gift and ivory tulle into the bag.

for the brown bag:
14" of ⅝" wide green/brown striped grosgrain ribbon
9" of ⅜" wide sage green grosgrain ribbon
9" of ⅜" wide dark brown grosgrain ribbon
4"x5" brown craft paper gift bag with handles
tissue papers: dark green, ivory
low temperature glue gun, glue sticks

Wrap the striped ribbon vertically around the front and back of the **brown bag,** gluing the ribbon ends to the inside. Hold the other ribbons together and tie into a shoestring bow, then glue it to the top front. Insert a gift and tissue paper inside the bag.

for the lavender bag:
28" of 1½" wide white satin ribbon
32" of ¾" wide purple/lavender satin striped sheer ribbon
5"x9" lavender gift bag with handles
white tissue paper
low temperature glue gun, glue sticks

Cut 10" from each ribbon, layer the striped ribbon onto the white and glue them to the left front of the **lavender bag.** From the remaining ribbons, make a white shoestring bow with 2" loops and 3½" tails, then a striped bow with 1½" loops with 6" and 8" tails. Cut an inverted "V" into each white tail. Trim each striped tail at an angle, then knot each near the end. Glue the striped bow to the white, then glue it to the bag top. Insert a gift and tissue into the bag.

for the green bag:
2 yards of 1⅜" wide green sheer ribbon with gold edges
one 4" cluster of lavender silk flowers with many ¾" wide blossoms and ½" wide berry clusters and 1" green leaves
5"x9" green pin striped gift bag with handles
purple tissue paper
24-gauge wire
wire cutters
low temperature glue gun, glue sticks

Glue an 18" length of ribbon horizontally around the center of the **green bag.** Tie the remaining ribbon into an oblong bow with a center loop, two 2½", four 3½" loops and two 4½" tails with an inverted "V" cut into each tail. Glue the bow to the bag front. Cut the floral stem in half and glue one above and below the bow. Insert a gift and tissue into the bag.

38

Wrap 2" wide lavender sheer ribbon around opposite corners of the **green package,** gluing the ends at the back. Use 1¾ yards of ribbon to make a puffy bow with eight 4" loops and no tails. Glue the bow to the top left corner. Cut sprigs from a purple silk hydrangea stem with five-six clusters of 1" wide blossoms and many 2"–3½" green leaves, then glue them among the bow loops.

Wrap 1½" wide yellow/green striped ribbon around the left and right sides of the **green package** and 1½" wide yellow/green floral ribbon around the center. Center an 18" length of the floral ribbon under the center ribbon, then tie the ends onto the ribbon into a shoestring bow with 2" loops and 3½" tail. Cut an inverted "V" into each tail.

Green package is 14½"x11"x3¼"

Wrap 2½" wide white sheer ribbon with wire edges around the sides of a **teal package.** Use 3¼ yards of ribbon for a puffy bow with a center loop, eight 3" loops and one 29" tail to wrap around the top and bottom of the package. Glue the bow over the side-wrapped ribbon, gluing the tail end under the bow. Glue two stems of white silk calla lily picks extending out opposite ends of the bow.

Baby socks and satin ribbons make a **baby shower gift** in this teal package a hit. Use 2⅓ yards of ⅞" wide teal geometric ribbon for a puffy bow with with a center loop, twelve 3" loops and two 3½" tails. Use Glue Dots™ to attach the socks so they can easily be removed. Wrap geometric ribbon and double-face satin ribbons around the sides.

Teal package is are 13"x12½"x1½"

Gift wrap: Changing the ribbon and embellishments with solid color gift wrap changes the look desired for the occasion. Packages come in all sizes and shapes. We've given the length needed for these two sizes.

These **mini white boxes** make whimsical little surprises when wrapped in ribbon. To wrap the ribbon around each box: Place the box upside down and centered on the ribbon. Pull the ribbon ends to the box center, twist once, then pull to opposite sides, turn the box upright and pull the ends to the center top of the box. Thread a charm onto one ribbon end, then tie the ends into a shoestring bow with 1½" loops and 2½" tails. Knot each tail ½" from the end, then trim each end at an angle.

1 yard of ¼" wide pink gingham ribbon
1 yards of ⅜" wide pink/white ombre ribbon
32" of ⅜" wide pink sheer ribbon with vertical stripes
silver charms: ½" tall pink heart, ¾" wide "Token of Love" medallion, ¾" wide pair of bells
white paper jewelry boxes: 3½" square, 8¼"x2" long rectangle, 3¼"x2¼" rectangle

You know there must be a special gift inside this **ribbon handle gift box**. The sheer ribbon handle adds a sophisticated appeal to the floral embellished lid.

32" of ¼" wide pink gingham ribbon
1¾ yards of ⅝" wide pink sheer ribbon with iridescent edges
2¾"x4½" ivory oval papier mâché box
white silk floral pick with three 2" wide blossoms and two 2½" green leaves
24-gauge wire
wire cutters
low temperature glue gun, glue sticks

One: Cut 14" from the sheer and gingham ribbons, glue the gingham centered on the sheer length, then glue the sheer ribbon onto the lid side. Cut a 10" length of sheer ribbon and glue one end to each lid end to form a handle. Cut the remaining gingham ribbon in half, tie each length into a shoestring bow and glue one to each lid end.

Two: Cut the flowers and leaves from the stem. Glue the leaves fanning out on top of the lid.

Three: With the remaining sheer ribbon, make a loopy bow with eight 2" loops and two 2" tails. Trim each tail at an angle, then glue the bow to the left side of the leaves. Glue the blossoms centered on the bow and leaves.

You know she's had one of those weeks. So, why not surprise her with a **ribbon-wrapped gift basket**. Insert aromatic bath gel, a net sponge and a ribbon-wrapped candle into the basket to say "relax."

3 yards of 2" wide yellow sheer ribbon
1 yard of 1" wide ivory sheer ribbon with woven edges
7"x11½"x5½" wicker basket with 8" tall handle
three 4" wide yellow silk roses, each with two clusters of 2"–3" green leaves
clear iridescent shredded filler
white cloth-covered 24-gauge wire
wire cutters
low temperature glue gun, glue sticks
bath supplies: bath gel, yellow net sponge, ivory candle in frosted glass

One: Cut the blossoms and leaf clusters from the stems. Glue the blossoms in a row across the front of the basket. Glue the leaf clusters extending outward from behind the blossoms.

Two: Cut 1 yard from the yellow ribbon. Glue one end to a handle base, then wrap the ribbon around the handle to reach the other side. Use the remaining yellow ribbon to make an oblong bow with a center loop, two 2" loops, four 3" loops and two 4" tails. Cut an inverted "V" into each tail. Glue the bow to the front handle base above the roses.

Three: Place the candle centered on the ivory ribbon, pull the ends to the top and tie into a shoestring bow with 2" loops and 3½" tails. Trim each tail at an angle. Insert the shredded filler and accessories into the basket.

When invited to dinner, it's thoughtful to bring a gift. An **organza bottle bag** is sure to impress the hostess. Insert the bottle into the bag, pull the drawstrings and tie into a shoestring bow. Wrap a 15" length of 1½" wide ivory sheer ribbon around the bottle neck and tie the ends into a shoestring bow with 2" loops and 3" tails. Cut an inverted "V" into each tail. Glue a 1½" wide organza ribbon rose to the bow center. Tie a "Thank You" tag around the bottle neck with a 12" length of ¼" wide white satin ribbon.

Cards

Invite your guests to a baby shower with a **baby card** wrapped in gingham ribbon.

18" of ¼" wide pink/white gingham ribbon
Sarabooks™ Amethyst Paper Pack for dark blue netting, light blue netting and blue textured label
cardstocks: pink, white
5"x6½" white card
2¼" blue gingham bunny applique
2 silver mini brads
⅛" hole punch
black ink pen
glue stick

One: With the fold at the left, cover the card front with dark blue netting paper. Cut a 5½"x2½" light blue netting rectangle, then tear along the top edge. Glue the rectangle to the bottom of the card front.

Two: Cut a 2"x2⅛" white cardstock rectangle, then mat it onto pink cardstock with a ⅛" border. Glue the bunny to the rectangle, then glue the rectangle centered on the top portion of the card front.

Three: Cut the ribbon to one 9", one 5½" and two 2¾" lengths. Glue the 5½" length across the card top. With the 9" length, make a shoestring bow with ¾" loops and 1" tails, then glue it to the left end of the top ribbon. Write "Baby" on the label, then punch a hole into each end of the label. Thread 1" of a 2¾" ribbon through each hole, folding it onto the top, then secure it with a brad. Glue the label and ribbon tails centered on the card front bottom as shown.

Tie it all together with an **all-occasion card** and striped grosgrain ribbon. No matter what the message, it'll be well received!

16" of ⅝" wide pink/yellow/green/blue striped grosgrain ribbon
Paper Pizazz® papers: *Mixing Soft Patterned Papers* for pink/green plaid (also by the sheet)
white cardstock
5"x6½" white card
⅜" wide flower charms: 1 yellow, 1 pink
2 silver mini brads
X-acto® knife, cutting surface
Mini Glue Dots®
glue stick

One: With the fold at the top, tear ¾" along the front bottom edge. Cut a 6¼"x3¾" plaid rectangle, tearing one long edge. Glue the rectangle centered on the card front.

Two: Cut a 6½"x1½" strip of white cardstock, tearing along the long edges. Glue a 6½" length of ribbon centered on the strip. Use the remaining ribbon to make a shoestring bow with 1" loops and 1½" tails. Cut an inverted "V" into each tail, then glue the bow centered on the strip.

Three: Use the X-acto® knife to cut a 1/16" slit into the ribbon, ¾" on each side of the bow. Insert the prongs of a brad through a charm ring, then insert the brad into the slit and fold the ends at the back of the strip. Glue the strip centered on the card front.

See inside the back cover for instructions on covering the card front.

Present someone special with a **"for you" card** to celebrate them!

10" of ¾" wide lavender embossed satin ribbon
Paper Pizazz® papers: *Soft Tints* for lavender diamonds on pin
5"x6½" white card
set of 3 self-adhesive gift packages and "for you" tag appliques
metallic gold pen
metal-edge ruler
X-acto® knife, cutting surface
glue stick

One: With the fold on the left, glue a 4¾"x6¼" lavender diamonds rectangle centered on the card front. Lightly draw a 2¼"x2½" rectangle centered 1⅜" below the top edge of the card front. Open the card onto a cutting surface and use the X-acto® knife to cut out the rectangle for a window. Then use the ruler to draw a gold border along the window edge.

Two: Cut a 6" length of ribbon. Wrap ½" of the left end around the card fold to the card back and glue in place. Wrap the right end to the card front inside and glue in place. Knot the remaining ribbon onto the ribbon border, then cut an inverted "V" into each tail.

Three: Attach the tag to the card front below the bow. Attach the packages to the card inside, centered inside the window.

Show your love with special touches on a **"With Love" card.** Chalking, inking and crumpling add subtle texture to showcase the striped ribbon on the tag.

12" of ¾" wide lavender/purple striped satin/sheer ribbon
Sarabooks™ Amethyst Paper Pack for purple sponged, lavender textured and purple textured tag
5"x6½" white card
purple decorating chalk
black ink pad
4 silver mini brads
⅛" hole punch
foam adhesive tape
glue stick
tracing paper, transfer paper
black ink pen or computer and printer

One: With the fold at the top, cover the card front with purple sponged paper. Use a computer and printer or handwrite "With Love" in the upper right corner of a 5½"x3¾" rectangle of lavender textured paper, then tear along the edges. Use the chalk to cover over the words, then press the torn edges of the rectangle onto the black ink pad and let dry.

Two: Punch a hole in each corner of the rectangle, insert a brad into the hole and fold the prongs flat on the back. Glue the rectangle centered on the card front.

Three: Cut out the tag and punch a hole at the top. Trace the heart pattern, then layer transfer paper on top of purple sponged paper with the traced pattern on top and retrace the heart. Cut out the heart from the purple sponged paper, crumple it, reflatten it, then attach it to the tag with foam tape. Thread the ribbon through the tag hole, knot it, then twist the tails and glue in place on the card front.

Cards

Express your gratitude with a black and white ribbon bow **thank you card**.

10" of ⅛" wide white stitches on black ribbon
24" of 1½" wide black/white gingham ribbon
Sarabooks™ *Ivory Paper Pack* for textured tan, brown script, onyx glimmer paper
Paper Pizazz® papers: *Alphabet Tiles* for black typewriter alphabet tiles (also available by the sheet)
5"x6½" white card
foam adhesive tape
glue stick

One: With the card fold at the top, cover the card front with brown script paper. Fold the gingham ribbon in half, place the fold centered on the card fold and glue the ribbon to the card front and back, allowing the ends to fall loose below the card bottom. Cut an inverted "V" into each tail.

Two: Cut a 4¼"x2½" rectangle of tan textured paper and mat it on black glimmer paper with a ⅛" border. Cut the grosgrain ribbon in half. Glue one length to the rectangle, ¼" from the top edge, wrapping the ends to the back. Repeat for the bottom.

Three: Cut out alphabet tiles to spell "THANK YOU". Attach them to the tan rectangle with foam tape. Glue the rectangle centered on the card front. Tie the gingham ribbon into a shoestring bow.

Wave the flag with ribbons for a patriotic message with the **USA card**. It's a great way to honor someone in the military!

28" of ¼" wide red/white gingham ribbon
Sarabooks™ *Ivory Paper Pack* for tan stars
Paper Pizazz® papers: *Tag Art* for American flag tags, eagle crest, USA alphabet tiles
5"x6½" white card
⅜" wide star charms: 1 ivory, 1 blue
three ⅛" red eyelets
eyelet setting tools
foam adhesive tape
glue stick
Mini Glue Dots®

One: With the fold at the left, cover the card front with tan stars paper. Cut out the tags and eagle crest. Glue the tags to the card front as shown. Use foam tape to attach the crest centered on top of the tags.

Two: Cut out the alphabet tiles to spell "USA," then glue them along the bottom of the card front. Open the card and attach an eyelet to the top of each tile.

Three: Wrap the ribbon around the fold of the card and tie the ends into a shoestring bow, 1½" from the top edge. Thread a charm onto each tail, 1" from the end and knot it in place. Trim each tail at an angle.

See inside the back cover for instructions on covering the card front.

Express your happiness for the bride and groom with this ribbon-wrapped **wedding day card.**

One: Cut 4½"x6" rectangles from white cardstock and yellow floral paper. Glue the rectangles together. With the floral paper on top, glue one end of the ribbon to the lower left back corner of the rectangle. Wrap the ribbon to the front, around the right side, across the back and to the front to make an "X" as shown, then repeat two more times. Glue the piece centered on the card front.

Two: Use a computer and printer or handwrite "Wedding Day" on white cardstock, then tear around the words into a 2½"x1" rectangle. Chalk the edges brown, then tuck the rectangle under one of the lower ribbons and glue in place.

Three: Glue the bouquet centered on the top portion of the card front.

60" of ¼" wide ivory sheer ribbon
Paper Pizazz® papers: *Flowered "Handmade" Papers & Vellum* for yellow handmade flowers (also by the sheet)
white cardstock
5"x6½" white card
3" tall ivory ribbon-wrapped paper rose bouquet
brown decorating chalk
black ink pen or computer and printer
glue stick

Make their day extra special with this **happy birthday card.** The ribbon-tied tags add a whimsical touch to the vellum pocket.

20" of ⅜" wide white sheer ribbon with satin edges
5" of ⅞" wide white satin ribbon
Paper Pizazz® papers: *Joy's Vintage Papers* for lavender stripes; *12"x12" Pastel Vellum Papers* for pastel purple vellum (also by the sheet); *Tag Art* for pressed flower tags
lavender cardstock
5"x6½" white card
four ⅛" white eyelets
eyelet setting tools
⅛" hole punch
foam adhesive tape
glue stick

One: With the fold at the left, cover the card front with stripes paper. Cut a 2¾"x3⅝" rectangle of vellum, measure ¾" down from the top right corner and cut diagonally between the top left corner and measured point on the right side of the rectangle. Open the card, place the vellum centered on the card front and attach an eyelet in each corner to form a pocket.

Two: Cut out the flower tags, then punch a hole at the top of each tag. Cut a 10" length of sheer ribbon. Thread the ribbon halfway through the hole in the large tag and knot. Thread one tail through the hole in the round tag and tie a knot 1½" from the end. Knot the other tail 1" from the end, then trim each tail at an angle. Insert the large tag into the vellum pocket, then use foam tape to attach the round tag to the pocket outside.

Three: Cut the remaining sheer ribbon in half and glue one length, ¼" from the top and bottom of the card front. Glue the satin ribbon to the card front, 2" from the bottom edge. Use a computer and printer or handwrite "Happy Birthday" across a 5"x⅝" strip of lavender cardstock. Glue the strip centered on the satin ribbon.

27" of ½" wide orange/yellow gingham ribbon with light pink and magenta edges
Paper Pizazz® papers: *12"x12" Soft Tints* for pink swirl, yellow dots (also by the sheet), pink checks
cardstocks: white, dark yellow
tracing paper
transfer paper
foam adhesive tape
¼" hole punch
glue stick

Gingham ribbon adds a fun texture to the **"When I Grow Up" scrapbook page.** Mat a 8½"x7¾" rectangle of yellow dots on white cardstock with a thin border. Glue a matted photo even with the right edge of the dots rectangle, then glue the piece to the right edge of the pink checks paper. Use a computer and printer or handwrite a message on a 4¾"x2½" rectangle of yellow cardstock and mat it on white with a thin border. Cut the ribbon to 15", 8" and 4". Wrap the 15" length along the left side of the page to form a border, gluing the ends at the back. Knot the center of the 4" length and glue it to the top of the message. Trace the hearts shapes onto yellow dots and pink swirls papers, mat each on white and punch a hole at the top. Knot the center of the 8" ribbon onto the ribbon border, 2½" from the top edge. Thread a heart onto each tail and tie a knot 1" from the end. Trim each tail at an angle. Use foam tape to attach the hearts to the page.

1 yard of ⅛" wide white stitches on red grosgrain ribbon
Paper Pizazz® papers: *Bright Great Backgrounds* for blue star burst; *Tag Art* for flag, eagle tags, *Tags Template*
cardstocks: navy blue, white
four 5⁄16" brushed nickel brads
⅛" hole punch
fine point black pen
clear adhesive tape
glue stick

Red ribbon accents add a fanciful touch to this **"Made in the U.S.A." scrapbook page.** Mat the photo on a thin white border, a 1" wide blue star burst and once more with a thin white border. Punch a hole centered on each side of the star burst mat and insert a brad into the top and side holes. Glue the top half of the photo mat centered slightly near the top of the navy cardstock sheet. Cut the ribbon into four 9" lengths. Wrap the center of one length around the top and side brads, spread the ends 1" apart and tape to the back. Punch a hole at the top of each tag, line up the holes over the bottom hole on the photo mat, then insert the brad into the hole. Slide the remaining ribbon under the tags and around the brad and pull the ends to the page bottom as with the other ribbon ends. Use the template to cut a tag from white cardstock, write your message on the tag, then glue it tucked between the tags. Glue the tags in place.

28" of ½" wide purple/white plaid satin ribbon
Paper Pizazz® papers: *Mixing Soft Patterned Papers* for lavender daisies, yellow/green stripes
cardstocks: sage, lavender, white
1½" wide circle tag with metal rim
number rubber stamps
black ink pad
fine point black pen or computer and printer
glue stick

Purple plaid ribbon adds a magical touch to this **"Fairy Princess" scrapbook page.** Glue a 5½"x12" rectangle of purple daisies and a 12"x8" rectangle of stripes paper to the lavender cardstock as shown. Use a computer and printer or handwrite your message on lavender, mat it on white, then glue it near the upper right corner of the stripes rectangle. Mat one photo on white and sage cardstock, each with a 1/16" border. Repeat the white border for a smaller photo. Glue the large photo near the upper left corner of the page and the small photo to the bottom of the stripes rectangle. Cut the ribbon to one 6" and two 12" lengths. Fold ½" of one 12" ribbon length to the left side back of the page, 2¼" above the bottom edge and glue it in place. Repeat with the 6" ribbon length for the right side of the page, tying a single knot into the ribbon ends. Slide the tag string hanger onto the knot, then knot the ribbon ends once more. With the remaining ribbon, make a shoestring bow with 1" loops and 1½" tails. Glue the bow above the message. Trim each set of ribbon tails at an angle. Use the rubber stamps and ink pad to stamp the year onto the tag.

15" of ⅝" wide blue/purple/tan satin-striped sheer ribbon
12" of ⅜" wide navy blue ribbed satin ribbon
10" of ⅜" wide teal/white double-faced satin ribbon with white stitch edges
Paper Pizazz® papers: *Flowered "Handmade" Papers & Vellum* for blue handmade flowers (also by the sheet)
cardstocks: teal, tan, white
fine point black pen or computer and printer
glue stick

Ribbons add textured to a **"Best Friends" scrapbook page.** Each photo features a variety of ribbon styles to keep the viewer's eye moving around the page.

Mat a vertical photo on teal and tan, each with a thin border. Mat a horizontal photo on tan, then teal with a ⅛" border along the top, bottom and left side and a 1" border on the right side. Wrap striped ribbon around the right side, gluing the ends at the back, then mat the piece on tan with a thin border. Knot the center of a 3" length of blue ribbon and glue it to the lower right corner of the photo mat. Use the computer and printer or handprint your message on white cardstock, then mat it on tan. Wrap teal ribbon around the top right corner. Knot the center of a 4" length of striped ribbon and glue it to the bottom. Wrap two 1½" lengths of blue ribbon from the top edge of the floral paper, then glue the message piece on top. Cut the remaining ribbons in 2"-3" lengths, trim each end at an angle and glue them as shown along the bottom of the vertical photo. Glue the photo to the left side of the page, then glue the horizontal photo slightly overlapping onto its lower right corner.

- 38" of ⅜" wide dark green ribbed satin ribbon
- Paper Pizazz® papers: *Joy's Vintage Papers* for green with white flowers, blue with green dots, blue lilies; *Tags Template*
- cardstocks: blue, sage, white
- 5" of gold thread
- 1/16" hole punch
- fine point black pen or computer and printer
- glue stick

Ribbon-wrapped photos add color and texture to the photos on this **"Gordy and LeNae" scrapbook page.** Mat each photo on blue with a ⅛" border. Cut two lengths of ribbon, knot each in the center, then wrap one around the bottom of each photo, gluing the ends at the back. Mat each photo (4"x6") on sage with a ⅛" border. Glue the photos at slight angles on the green floral paper as shown.

For the bottom border, tear along the tops of a 12"x2¾" blue lilies and a 12"x3¾" dots paper strips. Layer the lilies onto the dots paper and glue the pieces to the bottom of the page. Cut a 15" length of ribbon, knot it in the center and 2" from each end, then glue along the dots paper, gluing the ends at the back. Use the remaining ribbon to make a shoestring bow with 1" loops and 1½" tails, then glue it centered between the two left ribbon knots. Use a computer and printer or handwrite a message on white cardstock, then use the template to cut a tag shape surrounding the message, mat it on blue and punch a hole at the top. Tie the tag to the bow with the thread.

- 25" of ⅛" wide black squares on brown satin ribbon
- 8" of ¼" wide brown/ivory gingham ribbon
- 10" of ⅜" wide brown woven ribbon
- Paper Pizazz® papers: *Mixing Jewel Patterned Papers* for brown diamonds, brown/black tiles; *Alphabet Tiles* for black typewriter alphabet tiles
- cardstocks: black, brown
- Mini Glue Dots®
- foam adhesive tape
- glue stick

Woven ribbons add old-world charm to this **"1914" scrapbook page.** For the top border, cut a 12"x3" strip of the tiles paper and mat it on black cardstock, leaving a 1/16" border along the top and bottom. Cut the brown woven ribbon in half, then tie a knot in the center of each length. Wrap one length around each end of the tiles piece, gluing the ends to the back. Glue the tiles piece 1" from the top edge of the diamonds paper. Mat each photo (3½"x5½") on brown and black cardstock, leaving a ½" border of black cardstock on one mat. Wrap a 7" length of the black squares on brown ribbon on each side of the black mat, gluing the ends at the back.

Use the computer and printer or handwrite your message on a 4¼" brown square, mat it on black, then wrap the remaining black squares on brown ribbon around each side. Use foam tape to attach the number tiles onto a 3⅜"x1⅛" brown rectangle, mat it on black and glue it to the top border. Knot the gingham ribbon in the center, trim each tail at an angle, then glue it above the tiles.